Musings of the Northern Poet

poems of love and faith

- pocket edition -

by Matthew E Nordin

Musings of the Northern Poet

Copyright © 2020 by Matthew E. Nordin.

All rights reserved.

No part of this book may be used or reproduced, stored in or introduced into a retrieval system, or transmitted in any form whatsoever (electronic, mechanical, photocopying, recording, or otherwise) without prior written permission from the author except in the case of brief quotations, a bribery of coffee helps. For more information contact Matthew at matthewenordin@gmail.com.

Original edition published in 2016 by Dot's Micro-Publishing House, 29051 200 Road, Lebanon, Kansas 66952, www.dotsmicropublishinghouse.com. All rights returned to Author.

Cover design by author.

Musings of the Northern Poet: poems of love and faith (pocket edition)
ISBN: 978-1-7355573-1-1

Matthew E Nordin

TABLE OF CONTENTS

<u>PRELUDE</u>:
A Page Waits (2010)   1

<u>FAITH</u>:
A Work in Progress (2008)	4
Bricks and the Wall (2011)	5
Chains That Free Me (2010)	5
Corrupted Man (2007)	6
Despairing Storms (2009)	7
Each New Ending (2011)	8
Eternal Ocean (2008)	8
Finding Your Footing (2009)	9
Hope That Watches Us (2009)	10
Illuminate Glory (2011)	11
Incarnation (2003)	12
Learning Love (2006)	13
Memories Sprouting Seeds (2009)	14
My Cup of Tea (2008)	15
Naked in the Garden (2005)	16
Retraining Hands (2009)	17
Sign on the Wall (2010)	18
Soul Cry (2005)	19
That Sacrifice (2012)	19
That the World Will Believe (2007)	20
The Blossoms (2009)	21
The Transcendent/Immanent One (2005)	22
Tsidkenu (2008)	23
Undead Warrior (2003)	24
Vanity (2003)	25
We Wrestle Not (2001)	26
Weary Warrior (2001)	27
Weltanschauung Vessel (2008)	28

Musings of the Northern Poet

<u>LOVE</u>:

A Fresh Spin (2016)	30
An Angel's Ring (2009)	31
As I Wandered (2011)	31
As the Sun Warms (2011)	32
Content in Confusion (2008)	32
Contredanse of Memory (2011)	33
Dreaming Together (2010)	33
Endless Lines I Desire to Pen (2012)	34
Erato (2011)	35
Fragrance of Dreams (2009)	36
Hair Danced (2009)	37
Her Sweet Voice (2011)	38
I Choose to Love You (2011)	39
I Stop to Wonder at the Scene (2011)	39
I Watch the Moon Fall From the Skies (2011)	40
I Will Always Hold Your Heart (2011)	41
In Forest Deep by River Bank (2010)	42
Kiss Me Quickly (2010)	43
Never Alone Again (2009)	44
One Last Embrace (2011)	45
She Shines like the Stars (2008)	45
Sleep Sweetly Beside Me (2011).	46
Tell Me Again (2009)	46
The Bench's Edge (2012)	47
The Heartbeat That Lasts Forever (2010)	47
The I to We (2008)	48
What You Are to Me (2009)	49

<u>OTHER</u>:

A Proverb (2011)	52
A Simple Pardon (2009)	52
An Ode to Those in College Still (2010)	53
Breaking the Block (2011)	53
Kissed by Fire (2010)	54
Losing Ground (2009)	55

My Pen Let Loose (2010)	55
Nannwin (2011)	56
Ode in C (2012)	56
Old Year's Day (2011)	57
Reprise (2011)	57
Simple Moments (2010)	58
Snow of Two Thousand Ten (2010)	58-59
The Friar (2012)	60
The Insane Conclusion (2009)	61
The King's Army (2009)	62
The Seas of Eternity (2011)	63
These Stained Marks (2010)	64
To a Nettle Friend (2009)	65
Warming into Renaissance (2011)	65
What Makes a Warrior? (2009)	66
Wizard of Words (2009)	67

CONCLUSION:
My Mumbled Mind (2009)	69-71

Musings of the Northern Poet

Prelude

A Page Waits

A page waits for its staining words
Each stroke breathes life in the void space
Forming shadows of a lost soul
Only imagination's trace
The limits reach beyond our mind
Writing into another fate
Even when our marks have gone by
The ink's held in a timeless state
These woken lines and curves of life
Etched upon our memory's stone
Cling upon their canvas vessel
As with the page, we're not alone

Musings of the Northern Poet

Faith

"There is no saint without a past, no sinner without a future."
— Augustine of Hippo

Of all sinners, I find myself to be the worst as only I know my inner thoughts. Yet, thanks be to Jesus who forgives all and helps us live the true life. Be inspired and encouraged to the riches of His grace in the following lyrics.

A Work in Progress

I conclude I am a work in progress
The ungrateful and the prodigal son
Not focused on that which is beyond me
I hold on to the regrets I have done
Leaving a void that I once called my heart
The hole consumes all who would venture near
I ensnare all by my earthly desire
Searching to fill the scars of the past's fear

Yet, You came to make amends with my life
You whom I love and the One I entreat
You who will destroy the imperfections
And press me to advance by Your pierced feet
Until brought back to the family of faith
I realign my mind to seek Your face
My life overflows with Your holiness
As You illuminate my heart to race

This old flesh and its desires will soon fade
Love will remain and lift us from the mire
Our hearts will be filled with Your victory
Drowning in Your arms, consumed by Your fire

Matthew E Nordin

Bricks and the Wall

Brick
By brick
Run again
Shrugging off sin
I am halfway there
Love which none can compare
Built in peace that weathers pain
Breaking down walls of selfish gain
The path to Life has only begun
I squint my eyes as I reach for the Son

Chains That Free Me

I am compelled to proclaim love
Awakened by the Holy Dove
Descending to lift me again
Removing the decay of sin
Thinking I was hiding from You
I was already found in You
As a life comes from a dead seed
You have given me all I need
Lord, break me down so I can rise
With You and live in paradise
Capture me again in glory
Bind me with Your chains that free me
Laying down what hinders aside
For only in You will I hide
Until You shine in every part
Surrendering all for His heart

Corrupted Man

The worm infected drive
This virus in my head
Corroding the software
It will network and spread
The corrupted fragments
Make my memories a tool
Repeating the patterns
Of a life lived as fool

Wallowing with the dead
Can anything be new?
The demons I programed
Will soon reside in you

I must open my mind
Gouge out my shattered eyes
This dead soul is tainted
Kill the pain in my lies
Do not disdain the sick
For are they not like we?
If the sheep eat the sheep
Who then shall set us free?

Matthew E Nordin

Despairing Storms

Swirling clouds of doubt,
Despair
Lifting me in abysmal air
Shall I ever land?
Have I forgotten what it was like to stand?
Feeling only the cold rain
It numbs the other pain while I waste
Into a vortex of fear
Too many voices forcing me to hear
The noise brings chaos
Sounds shoving me around
My mind crumbles to my feet
My body reduced to mere raw meat
Diving for a fresh snack
The storm in a vulturous attack
Causes me to lose grip
I slip from my thoughts of love
Until my eyes catch a glint from above
The warmth of a Light breaks in
I feel an old smile form again
As the Son is breaking through
Reminding me
All things are made new
That Voice resounds, "I Am near"
The storm shakes with its own fear
Its constraint on me falters out
I am shattering the doubt
The Light surrounds me again
Releasing me from the fog of sin
Renewed by mercy and grace
I press forward to seek His face

Each New Ending

Why must we fear each new ending
Beginning to fill the skies
With sighs
Our woes rise in prayers unending
Sending those worries aside
Reside in His holy hand
Understand
His plan draws courage to abide
Alongside that life, love is twin
Within you'll join the throng
Prolong
The song that's waiting to begin
Again your prayers will be at peace
Increased by hope eternally
Foresee
The Jubilee that will release

Eternal Ocean

I float through this jaded culture of self
Knowing You bring the spring of endless wealth
Your words fill me like water in a fish
Drowning out the lonely and the selfish
Your water gives life to those who drink it
I stop my struggle to breathe Your Spirit
Letting the waves sway me to Love's motion
Established in that eternal ocean
Where the waters around are never still
As I'm submersed deeper into Your Will
And from that buoyancy You bring my soul
In my immersed life, I am transformed whole

Matthew E Nordin

Finding Your Footing

Struggling to open your eyes
After a drug induced sleep
Crawling from the bed of lies
Destruction is all you'll reap
Your feet step in their routine
As you stumble for the door
Darkness lures like nicotine
The sunlight you now abhor

How did this happen again?
The choice was not what it seems
A cough inside from the sin
While you abandoned your dreams
Too ashamed to show your face
The mirror will not forget
Scars that time cannot erase
As you wash off the regret

It was your soul you denied
The world's lies drug you away
But Love calls from the inside
There is no price you've to pay
You must turn to His glory
Repentant of all your sins
For the end of each story
Is when a new one begins

Musings of the Northern Poet
Hope That Watches Us

I fell on the streets of this town
Even the sunset drags me down
Been knocked under the city sewers
But I still find that love endures
When all the world seems dark and gray
Eyes can hardly see past today
There is a hope that watches us
And open arms that we can trust

I've tasted poison on my tongue
I thought the final note was sung
Blindly walked through my selfish fires
But found forgiveness never tires
When all the world seems dark and gray
Eyes can hardly see past today
There is a hope that watches us
And open arms that we can trust

You found me in my fallen state
And did not stop or hesitate
Now life is all I have to gain
I've been healed by a bloody stain
When all the world seems dark and gray
Eyes can hardly see past today
There is a hope that watches us
And open arms that we can trust

Illuminate Glory

This breath given to me
I cannot take it back
Why should I breathe any other way?

This path given to me
Will bring me to true life
Why should I stumble and fall away?

May my wisdom be found
Where Your grace doth abound
So may my words be true
And illuminate glory to You

Incarnation

Came down to sin
To live again
The God indivisible
Split just for a little while
To die for us
To live in us
Almighty incarnated
So we can abide in Him
His blood was shed
The payment dead
By true love's incarnation
God's greatest revelation
Do you know this God?
This God who came down
Do you know this man?
This man wore a crown
The crown of suffering
The crown of victory
Fully God and Fully man
Love's revealed mystery

Learning Love

I'm just a simple man with simple things
But You can make them great and my heart sings
I fear I'm wasting the time You gave me
Until I realize it's for Your glory
Don't want my own fame
My praises rise to You
Don't want to waste it
I give my time to You
Oh Lord, please help me
I'm learning how to love You

I sit to think as the day wanders by
Waiting here while a glaze protrudes my eye
I look to the day of eternity
When I shall forever give You glory
Don't want to fail You
I want to live for You
Don't want to bear it
I surrender to You
Oh Lord, please help me
I'm learning how to love You

Memories Sprouting Seeds

The memories fall like rotten fruit
As regret begins to take root
But I know these thoughts should not stand
I cast them out, quick as I can
New seeds sprout in the broken ground
Covering the pale ruins around
The vines scatter among the old
Leaves replace all the dust and mold
A graveyard of hearts crumbling
The healing is almost tumbling
Over the jagged scars of pain
I soak in the flood of Love's rain

Matthew E Nordin
My Cup of Tea

My mind wanders stirring my cup of tea
Have we been brainwashed by society
What happens when possessions possess us?
How can we not be consumed by our lust?
Apathetic shells of people survive
As culture feeds on consumers to thrive
Hope in children's eyes is replaced by tears
Dreams are forgotten by lies in their ears
Tearing out ideas that the pain will cease
They desperately grab for joy and peace
Wondering if it is worth it to be
Darkness is all they are able to see
The world hides that our image is the same
All of us were created in His Name
I see the problems cycle endlessly
Not only in the world but inside me
Where have I forsaken what I have learned?
How many times has my old self returned?
My own cup has been tainted by the past
Yet knowing only faith, hope, and love last
Old habits must be replaced by the new
Praying to be restored to what is true
For the Father gives us all that we need
Mercy comes as his wounds no longer bleed
I can only sip of the love He shows
While I lean back and my cup overflows

Naked in the Garden

I strive for peace in this world full of lies
A dream that bloomed leaves a hole where it dies
The seed of this flesh is rotten and old
Blinded by the regret, my heart grows cold
As the wicked seemed blessed while they are here
Consuming more friends, they lust for their beer
Their arrogant smiles fill with hopelessness
Praising porcelain gods of drunkenness

I try so hard to understand His grace
As the sweat of my brow drips in my face
But His Law has been written on my heart
The old seed destroyed as new species starts
My eyes close not until they see His Word
My works end not until His Name is heard
From the lips of all people, small and great
From those lost in sin to the weary saint

For my hearts is stilled when I speak His Name
Dreams resurrected, God Almighty came
He will mend this heart so tattered and frail
Rekindle the lost fire, sharpen the nail
Pierce the Holy Man, His blood covers sin
Kill the Spotless Lamb, He rises again
I have been freed, stripped from the sin again
I stand redeemed, naked in the garden

Matthew E Nordin
Retraining Hands

The sin drips off my fingers
While the fear still lingers
Death is all I can see
While the actions scream back at me
Pushing forward with broken feet
I know I should retreat
Following the wrong voice
Thinking it was all up to choice
Trying to remove a master
As the clock gets faster
I hear the sound again
An echoing song of a Friend
Point my feet to Your direction
Cleanse my fingers to perfection

Musings of the Northern Poet

Sign on the Wall

Filling lungs with smoke for a high
Thinking life has passed them by
Resting in a cold, lonely bed
The drugs swirling round their head
While a child gets lost outside
The beaten try to hide
A stomach full of worms
Our head barely turns
And the faded coke sign on the wall
Shows us just how far we'll fall
And I know it's not fair to say
That we might not live today
Yeah I know it's absurd to say
That we won't wake up today

And the stress that we take from work
Makes others see us as jerk
And so we drive our cars away
Thinking maybe we should pray
But the chair calls us again
The TV our old friend
A murder up the street
Sins of lazy feet
And we hang a new sign on the wall
Take heed where you stand or fall
And I know it's not fair to say
That we just might live today
Yeah I know it's absurd to say
That we could wake up today

18

Matthew E Nordin

Soul Cry

When the joys of life wither all away
And I cannot count Your blessings each day
I pray that You will strengthen me again
As I wait on Your timing to set in
Oh God I need You, Lord I praise You
I lift up my voice, as I lift up my life
Jesus, Spirit, Father, Master!
Almighty God, I give my life to You

There is a man who walked upon this earth
Who gave His life to give us a new birth
He gave His love to heal our brokenness
So who are we to give Him any less?
Oh God we need You, Lord we praise You
We lift up our voice, as we lift up our life
Jesus, Spirit, Father, Master!
Almighty God, we give our life to You

That Sacrifice

Oh that torch within my breast
Oh that peace which bids me rest
How I seek that still small voice
Echoing beyond that choice
That saved me from lofty pride
Setting me on glory's side
Daily dying to my sin
Raising up with Him again
By that sacrifice we live
Hope and love for all we give

Musings of the Northern Poet
That the World Will Believe

I'm done with the routine of wasting time
We need to wake up and let our Light shine
Don't be a candle that makes ample light
Burn like an inferno that cuts through night
Hold nothing back to every tongue, tribe, and nation
He longs for all of us to find His Salvation
Don't tarry too long only reading from His Word
Begin to live it out, let your actions be heard
For they don't know because we fail to pray
Pushing out humility for today
Instead we worry over this or that
While the birds and the lilies point and laugh
We joke about the poor, their children fill our streets
We speak of peace but never turn the other cheek
Shrapnel stricken cities, the death is in their beds
AIDS infested culture, the cancer's in our heads
Beat down your swords and throw away your gun
It's about time to let His Kingdom come
Buddhist, Muslim, Jewish, or Atheist
Christian, Liberal, gay, straight, or terrorist
The Bible does not label who we are to love
Get your eyes off yourself for God's the only Judge
Fueled by the Spirit, live life as a scream
That the world will believe God reigns supreme

Matthew E Nordin

The Blossoms

The blossoms form in season
By a set pattern ordained
A measurable circle
The force cannot be explained
The bees weave the tapestries
Yet worms rarely see the sky
Such beauty can be planned for
Even when the flowers die
But when the physical fails
And the last one falls in dirt
We will see them like shadows
As the curse has been subvert
In love, the cycles were formed
In rebellion, they felt death
Until beauty is restored
From our Love's renewing Breath

Musings of the Northern Poet
The Transcendent/Immanent One

Dripping with wisdom
Burning with mercy
Sparkling with justice
Yet still You hear me

Stronger than beauty
Greater than eyes see
Bigger than a dream
Yet still You love me

So how can I love
Someone transcendent?
Can I comprehend
Someone immanent?

When I fell from you
You reached out to me
Redeemed me from sin
And set my soul free

Matthew E Nordin

Tsidkenu

My life is a breath
Spoken by You, lived for You
My days are a breath
A mist that vanishes; a shadow that fades
So who am I
That you would die for me?
So what am I
That You set Your mark on me?
Such love I do not understand
Grace freely given; blood covered sin
I don't know the words to speak
My spirit praises Him, Jesus, Jehovah Tsidkenu

Undead Warrior

undead warrior
covered by the Blood
possessed by the Spirit
i rise from the dead

undead warrior
fighting to survive
a world that is broken
for i have true Life

undead warrior
trying to find rest
struggling with the darkness
i must battle on

undead warrior
with Joy as my strength
evil cannot touch me
my soul is not mine

undead warrior
fighting for the Blood
His death has given Life
i will make Him known

Matthew E Nordin

Vanity

Under the sun
Since time has begun
That which has been
Is that which will be
The more wisdom
The more grief
Increasing knowledge
Increasing pain
With all you make
You'll always want
With all you do
It's never enough
No lasting remembrance
Between wisdom and ignorance
It's all striving after none
Nothing new under the sun

Under the sun
What's the use of fun
That which has been
Is that which will be
The more pleasure
The more grief
Increasing effort
Increasing pain
Life is fleeting
You'll always want
Life is tragic
It's never enough
Temporary as blowing mist
Life's mercurial existence
Everything under the sun
Vanity, unless lived for the Son

We Wrestle Not

Was it the instinct inside us
That drives the adrenaline rush?
Our cursory lives fueled by nature's lies
Veil our eyes
In illusions of right
We kill for a fight

Why do we ignore Love's command?
Forged from the Rock on which we stand
It's the foundation of His salvation
Temptation
Still drives us to war
Yet as slaves no more
We live for the One we adore

Weary Warrior

Oh Lord, My sword started to rust
The things I owned have turned to dust
My heart, it grows weary
And my body fails me
When I falter You're always here
Yet still my doubt breeds fear
So retrain my focus
To live a life victorious

Too many times I've felt alone
Thinking this struggle is my own
But the battles I see
All end for Your glory
I know You said You're always here
And Your love drives out fear
So retrain my focus
To live a life victorious

Musings of the Northern Poet
Weltanschauung Vessel

I scrutinize life through my cozy ship
Enjoying the view with coffee to sip
In my vessel, I search for happiness
Embarked on a path that brings less distress
Although there are times when I feel confined
Greater sense is made from that which is behind

I watch other vessels pass by with care
Knowing there is judgment in their blank stare
They mock and they boast of their great success
While I refine my course to their progress
I have a device to hear what they say
As I keep what's good and throw bad away

But sometimes warnings get tossed out instead
And words of evil are echoed inside my head
Most injustice I can shake off to the side
Other things pierce and cause damage inside
Although the marks may cause truth to pass
The world makes more sense through filtered glass

Continuing through each and every hard trial
I wave with a casual, occasional smile
I've heard the voice of One who can repair
Yet I fear the change would leave my ship bare
If I went out, I wonder what I'd find
I fear there will be more ships like mine

Love

"Every heart sings a song, incomplete, until another heart whispers back. Those who wish to sing always find a song. At the touch of a lover, everyone becomes a poet."
— *Plato*

Each poem is a slice of my soul. In these small morsels, you could unlock the deeper passions inside of your own heart. May these be used to woo your dreams. Let the duet begin.

A Fresh Spin

Each day is a fresh spin around a star
Coiling toward eternity to unwind
Each day I can see how lovely you are
No one so precious could I ever find
Such beauty enraptures my very soul
The earth eclipsed by the light in your eyes
Forever dimmed by the two become whole
As we rotate together I realize
We are the image of glory divine
Our lives reflecting from the inner Son
Such a union when our love does entwine
Causes the world's desires to be undone
Clinging to a love that will never part
Leaves me breathless with no more words to say
Whirling together with heart holding heart
We twist closer together with each day

Matthew E Nordin

An Angel's Ring

Please do tell me sweet fae
Who you're charming today
Though I know what you'd say
I wish to go your way

Your hypnotic eyes sing
Do not turn a cold wing
Oh what joy it would bring
For you're an angel's ring

No man can find beauty
Like what my eyes now see
And heaven it would be
If you'd travel with me

As I Wandered

I skipped with the fresh leaves that day
When a fairy glittered my way
She danced and giggled at the sight
For this poet brought her delight
She seemed to speak only to me
As if our paths were meant to be
Such magic dwelt within her eyes
Her voice, even a sweet surprise
I knew at once our hearts belong
As we sang together Love's song

As the Sun Warms

As the sun warms upon your face
So shall I be lit by your grace
With eyes soft as a fawn asleep
That causes my essence to leap
For never beauty mine eyes see
Until they lighted upon thee

Content in Confusion

So close, hair tickles face
So real, mind can't erase
And each passing moment
Changes before we know it
Until the time has skipped
While the music slipped
Into a whole new song
Our fear will not last long
The mind begins to blow
As time begins to slow
Content in confusion
A passion transfusion
The tension seemed lighter
And the stars danced brighter
A tangled mess of friends
Where the future depends
On destined plans of God
That the angels applaud

Matthew E Nordin

Contredanse of Memory

The feelings linger on my lips
My spirit from my body slips
Dancing on as I reminisce
Every tingle of our first kiss
A collision of emotion
Divine design set in motion
Such passion pierced into my heart
In those moments our lives did start
Sealing a friendship that remains
Waiting until only Love reigns

Dreaming Together

Listen to my heart, my darling
Hear it beat for you
Take hold of my hand, my dearest
It is strong for you
Drift away in my eyes, my love
They burn bright for you
Be at peace in my mind, my sweet
Planning dreams for you

My darling, your heart is beating
Calling out to me
My dearest, your hand is reaching
Grasping on to me
Oh my love, your eyes are burning
Looking straight to me
My sweet, your mind has been dreaming
Bringing you to me

Musings of the Northern Poet
Endless Lines I Desire to Pen

Endless lines I desire to pen
A poem that would never end
As I attempt to describe you
I always find something new
With every mark upon this space
I fear that one can only trace
A brief portrait of who you are
Attempting to describe a star
Even stars fade to your beauty
Still brighter than our galaxy
Such illuminate waves of hair
Cascading in ribbons everywhere
While your eyes make my worlds stand still
Yet with a smile my heart does fill
Your beauty is an endless dream
Like camping by a quiet stream
Where we plunge in waters unknown
Learning how love is truly grown
Opening new depths to explore
An adventure forevermore

Erato

A poet should be wary
If he were to meet his muse
Destiny would be merry
As fated passion ensues
Ever lost in each one's eyes
Souls dancing in the windows
And together their heart cries
As laughter and peace follows
It's as if every love song
And every sonnet written
Found the right place to belong
Such fortune has now bitten
Indeed it did not take long
This poet has been smitten

Fragrance of Dreams

Rest your head upon my heart
Let the rhythm soothe your mind
May it beat out the day's heat
In sleep's comfort you will find
The troubles are left behind

Breathe in the fragrance of dreams
As the stars extend their hands
Friends are waiting on moonbeams
An oasis of night's sands
Release your thoughts to new lands

Let them carry you away
Or to home if you desire
Join imagination's play
Where your muscles never tire
As you enter mind's empire

May your eyelids remain closed
When you find that secret place
With serenity enclosed
And there is not gloomy face
Drifting to the night's embrace

Follow me into the deep
Where all things hold a surprise
Enjoying this sublime sleep
For tomorrow at sunrise
We must reopen our eyes

Matthew E Nordin

Hair Danced

'Twas ever in the month of May
That my heart was stricken for true
In that blissful moment I knew
I had finally found my today

Her eyes lit up my darkest day
While hair danced with the wind that blew
Her lips, sweeter than morning's dew
Pulled me in as I went her way

I barely had the strength to say
"Sweet heaven's angel, I love you"
As I spoke, everything was new
For love had taken us away

Her Sweet Voice

Of all the paths and pages turned
It seems of beauty I'm unlearned
For such just fluttered past my way
Such a muse one could never say
Her smile consumed me from afar
With hair that matched the brightest star
I know not how I became bold
To approach this vision untold
A spell she cast upon my feet
That caused my rhyming to be sweet
Refreshing like the morning's dew
From such sonnets are dreams made new
I must give my heart reprimand
For it is slipping from my hand
But alas, it has made its choice
To sing along with her sweet voice

Matthew E Nordin

I Choose to Love You

I love you because of who I am
and who I want to be
Together we have a future hope,
forever you're in me
Yet just as you are in me,
I am in you eternally
Two lives become one heart
beating in rhythm continually
Such timeless moments of grace
when I look into your beauty
No words could capture
even the slightest glance of what I see
Symphonies composed within my mind
explain our unity
And so I choose to love you
because of who you are to me

I Stop to Wonder at the Scene

I stop to wonder at the scene
Everything starts to lose its green
Soon to be wrapped in a white sheet
Where the brave few wander the street
Yet you and I will still remain
Exploring through the wind and rain
Growing the fresh new leaves of love
That many others just dream of
Holding fast as the evergreens
Focused on what love truly means

Musings of the Northern Poet
I Watch the Moon Fall from the Skies

I watch the moon fall from the skies
Half falling onto the cool ground
The other half lit in her eyes
Glitters of moon dust all around
I could never dream such a place
Fireflies floated in her hair
Then burned up with the stars in space
Leaving sparkles in the night air
That streaked into my joyful soul
Waiting for their spark to ignite
These lights of heaven knew their role
As they danced on into the night
And from this fairy field's summer bliss
With the most bittersweet goodbye
My heart exploded in her kiss
As the moon flung back to the sky

Matthew E Nordin

I Will Always Hold Your Heart

I will always hold your heart
Wherever I may be
For even if we're apart
You will remain in me
As a diamond always worn
Reflecting light inside
A friendship that's never torn
The one I can confide
For this miracle started
And cannot be undone
Death could not make us parted
Forever just begun
Hearts beating in harmony
A gift love must impart
And now etched eternally
A diamond in my heart

Musings of the Northern Poet
In Forest Deep by River Bank

In forest deep by river bank
There in the brook my fears they sank
She gazed into this heart of mine
And evermore it shall be thine

I was asleep upon the stream
My raft was drifting in a dream
Until I heard the softest sound
In fairest dreams could not be found

I woke at once with much delight
For from sweet sound came breathless sight
As forest's leaves played with her hair
I was held in my wishful stare

That's when her eyes lit in my soul
Fate's cup was spilling overfull
It was her song that moved within
I left my boat and jumped right in

As water kissed her lovely feet
It was in fate that we did meet
Like the waters consume the sea
Her heart had sought and captured me

As a soft brook upon the sand
And the sweet earth that holds its hand
Our lives are one, now together
And flowing on to forever

Matthew E Nordin

Kiss Me Quickly

Just in case the skies start to fall
Kiss me before I go
Tell me of what I know
How our love endured through it all
This love ignited both our hearts
Our path together set
In fate's greatest moment
Each renewed day our journey starts
And at last we are here
Guided by love that drives out fear

Never Alone Again

The grass turned green with the Spring's air;
The meadows drank up the sweet rain.
The trees shook off the winter's pain
When we found that our love was there.

"Never alone again, again.
Never alone again," she said.
"I have a peace inside my head.
See me never alone again."

The stars stand still when our hands meet;
The thunders break forth with their song.
Why did we have to wait so long
To share each one's life now complete?

"Never alone again, again.
Never alone again," she said.
"I have a peace inside my head.
See you never alone again."

For six great years we still begin
To find that our love is still new
And this be our song, dancing true:
"We are never alone again."

"Never alone again, again.
Never alone again," she said.
"I have a peace inside my head.
See us never alone again."

One Last Embrace

The last page of their story
Concluding their long journey
He whispers into her ear
Assuring her not to fear
Rolling back to face the sky
They smile at the years gone by
His health would wander away
But by his side she would stay
She grabs his hand once again
They know new life will begin
All eternity to share
With no pain or tears to bare
They start to slip into bliss
Turning for their final kiss
Hair falls again in his face
As they share one last embrace

She Shines like the Stars

If stars could shine like my lady
They'd align with her gravity
Dancing about her in great swirls
Bringing light to entire worlds
She blazes forth without a sound
I find warmth when she is around
Too brilliant for one to stare long
Yet it is right where I belong
I will spin my life around hers
As a dazzling love occurs

Musings of the Northern Poet
Sleep Sweetly Beside Me

Sleep sweetly beside me, my darling love
Let blankets from heaven hold you above
The troubles and pains of the waking world
And become lost in your dreams now unfurled
Pausing briefly as you bring me along
As we embark again on slumber's song
The track curls through our imagination
Charted to an unknown destination
Where the when and how become forgotten
And all our memories never grow rotten
Where they are relived again and again
Even the ones that could never begin
For as we ride aboard this train's lost flight
With you, my darling love, we find true light

Tell Me Again

Tell me again how you love me
 So these wings of mine may fly free
No bird has ever seen this place
Reaching beyond the deepest space
Where new stars form and swirl around
The stream where no pain can be found
We float on this moonlight river
That continues past forever

Matthew E Nordin

The Bench's Edge

Sitting on a park bench one afternoon
We talked about our plans coming soon
If we should take the long way around
Or never let our feet touch the ground
Being caught up in something heavenly
A love that most cannot even see
We share the past to grow together
We share our dreams that now take feather
Lifting us from our grounded seat
Forcing us to run on bare feet
Onto the shores of life's purpose
We dive into its wild surface

The Heartbeat That Lasts Forever

A glance across the room's all it takes
A flash of hair, the curve up of lips
The heart beats faster as the time shakes
When a second lingering look slips
And then you are frozen together
In the heartbeat that lasts forever
The brain stops as you search for a sound
But the words remain just out of place
And then the world spins faster around
Maybe it was something on your face
As their eyes wander to another
Yet you can't forget the spark that met
And though your hopes begin to smother
It's too late for fate to let you forget

The I to We

It was a subtle change I couldn't miss
A death to myself in each kiss
I couldn't feel myself falling apart
As you harmonized in my heart
At that time, I was enlightened to love
The kind I had merely dreamed of
When my ego had a massive attack
My needs and wants became pushed back
And as you stepped forward to take their place
The transformation hit our face
We can no longer be defined alone
For when we're together, it's home
The I destroyed to be replaced by we
Us has become what people see
A unity reaching past perception
Dual lives revealing deception
The hidden confusion now brought to sense
Darkness lightened up through presence
You pushed me away to bring out the we
Giving way for us to be free

Matthew E Nordin

What You Are to Me

You are the song in my sleep
That I long for when I wake
The melody is too deep
Physical music can't make

You are the fire in my heart
That keeps it forever warm
A flame only God could start
A consuming passion storm

You are that new Autumn breeze
That breaks the tension of heat
Allowing my mind to ease
Drifting me off of my feet

You are a wondrous garden
For all those who seek beauty
Although the door is hidden
You have opened up to me

You are that familiar room
Where you truly feel at home
Serenity is in bloom
Even if you try to roam

You are the perfect art piece
That all would long to display
Where the critic's remarks cease
And breaths are taken away

You are a book to open
I anticipate each page
Reading words freshly spoken
Freeing ideas from their cage

Musings of the Northern Poet

Other Poetry

"I like this place and could willingly waste my time in it."
— William Shakespeare

Some of these are themed while others are ramblings—a soliloquy for the muses. I hope you find joy in the rants of this madman. After all, a differing perspective is what makes us all uniquely human.

Musings of the Northern Poet

A Proverb

I will attempt to write
But it is all in vain
Everything progresses
Everything decays
Everything changes
Everything stays
A pointless proverb
Of worthless words
Let not your life
Be the same

A Simple Pardon

My mind was so entwined
With faeries and rhymes
They cast a spell
And I fell
To dust
Trust
They're just
Words of sand
Pray understand
It did not make sense
Please pardon my offense

Matthew E Nordin

An Ode to Those in College

Frantic faces of students studying
Treacherously typing their weary work
The future is at stake!
Pour pleasures of caffeinated coping
Avoid annoyances where learners lurk
Please just give them a break!

Breaking the Block

I drag my pen through this dry block
That has captured my muse in lock
Struggling for the inspiration
As deplorable thoughts consume
Searching for one that speaks to soul
Breaking all down to make one whole
The ink drips out revelation
As the art breaks out of its tomb
Imagination bursts inside
I should set my tea to the side

Kissed by Fire

The people slowly gathered 'round
As the drumming let out it's sound
Through smoke and ashes they've traversed
The rhythm and movements rehearsed
Their heartbeat pulses with the drums
Drink from the flask where the fire comes
The blaze will leave you in a trance
If you carefully watch their dance
Floating orbs on a skin so fair
The beat continues with such care
You find yourself moving along
The crowd sways with the ancient song
Though the rain tried to wash it out
The players let their torches shout
For even after they've all gone
The charred memories linger on

Matthew E Nordin

Losing Ground

Each knight took his side
Waiting for the trumpet's call
Each knight rode forward
Hoping the other would fall

Crowds cheered at a blow
That sent one to losing ground
Crowds gave them new strength
As the threatening swords resound

In a yielding stance
Dishonorable blood spilt
In a vengeful strike
A sword is plunged to the hilt

My Pen Let Loose

My pen let loose your mystic art
With hope and wisdom to impart
Use your old ink in words and rhyme
To be a light in this dark time
Show beauty of Creative One
As flowers open to the sun
Relight that fresh fire to explore
Let our waking dreams long for more
Restore in us our lost children
Filling our imagination
Fill in the lines to make us whole
Together singing with our soul

Nannwin
(in memory of Clifford Williams II "Nannwin")

Another hurt, biting pain
A soul lifted from this place
Leaving a dull empty stain
That reflects from heart to face
So much friendship left unknown
So much time we must now wait
Yet now you have fully grown
And even if time seems late
We will meet you on that day
When all the hurt and pain cease
When all stains get washed away
Joining you in perfect peace

Ode in C

Of all the letters I see
I find you most unnesessary
I kan still make sense without you
The sounds I need kome through
So what is your point "C"
If you do not affekt me
Sure the spelling seems korrupted
But you must be abdukted
For you annoy me most
How you konstantly boast
The kurve of your letter
I like my lines better
So stay out of my rhyme
I'll change it next time

Matthew E Nordin

Old Year's Day

As this new year comes to an end
The ink creeks as pine from my pen
So much captured in thought and word
So many moments have been heard
It's a year that laughter lightened
It entertained and enlightened
We now sit slowly in our seat
With the moon's cycles now complete
Some friends fell while the others bloomed
Some walked away and others swooned
The poets, fairies, and mages
Even pirates became sages
And as we close this year's story
We reflect upon our journey
Memories now of fairies and friends
Wait for the sun as this night ends

Reprise

Their travels have come to an end
With new memories and new friends
The ship secure for a season
Until the sun warms a reason
For the dreamers to rise from bed
Lighting up with the black and red
As the Winter's night creeps along
So we must reprise at the song
To this year, we say our farewell
That graced us with stories to tell
New adventure waits for Spring air
We shall meet again at next Faire

Musings of the Northern Poet

Simple Moments

The wind in the vines
Rhythms in the breeze
Dancing and singing
Sounds to bring you ease
The notes of this life
Are played in sonnets
That follow a song
Captured in time's nets
One can only sip
Of simple moments

Snow of Two Thousand Ten

The world has been turned upside down
As the first snow falls to the ground
I bundle up in warmer skin
And let this adventure begin
Forging through streets where most slide past
Through the building white that won't last
I hear summer's reeds bend and snap
As they retire for a cold nap
I witness a seed lose its grip
The ice causes its strength to slip
I catch a lonely sensation
With the statue's meditation
And one set of feet leave a mark
As I walk through this empty park
But the city's glow lights my way
While a rabbit hops out to play
Yet even the geese with white back
Provide not a delicate quack

Matthew E Nordin

They dare not disturb the silence
With an unwanted noise violence
The water shivers with each drop
As the snow's moment makes time stop
I look over the misty lake
Healing inside begins to shake
The flakes alight and disappear
I pause to hit a tree once dear
Trying to think of season's past
How the darker days did not last
I turn down the path and retrace
Where the snow begins to erase
But the marks in my mind remain
Frosting over most of the pain
And this cold night in November
Froze in moments I'll remember
For someday I'll come back again
To this snow of two thousand ten

The Friar
(Written for Joseph, our Ren Faire "Friar")

Oh Friar
Come take me higher
One so religious
Thick as a deciduous
Such massive joy
Funny and coy
With his big stick
And a quick flick
He is a rotund man
Many visits to the frying pan
Boisterous as a donkey
He can be quite zonkey
Yet he pleases the masses
A tongue sweet as molasses
Now a worthy knight
But he will not bite
Few could be so courageous
And remain outrageous
This dancer for all
Could be summed up as "AAAHHH"
For he shall never tire
The one, and only, our Friar

Matthew E Nordin
The Insane Conclusion

The insanity of obsession
Makes us go back again and again
Trying to reach a higher goal
But enticed by the simple sin
The insanity mixed our love and hate
There is no more balance to be found
Forever lost in a run-on
The sentence loops us back around
The insanity stripped us
All hope found null
The ink has run dry for us
The paper full
The insanity of bittersweet
Memories too broken to abuse
Our last words were spoken apart
But it was just the same old news
This insanity is now over
This insanity at last did cease
Again and again we seek Him
Again and again we find peace

The King's Army

Can you feel the marching footsteps?
Can you hear the battle cry?
Can you see the flock of arrows
As they blacken out the sky?
Won't pierce courage of commanders
For their hearts beat steady on
Their armor shines through the darkness
Even though they've struggled long
Their swords are ready to take blood
And are sharpened ever true
In the hands of skillful soldiers
They will never break in two
Though the battle has just started
The victor is decided
No foe can stop this army when
Their minds are undivided

Matthew E Nordin

The Seas of Eternity
(for Kayleen Amos 12/31/1989 – 08/09/2011)

Where does the light of candles go
After they have been smothered out?
Where does the last sound escape to
After the echoes of a shout?
Do these final sound and light waves
Continue through eternity?
Where goes the memory of a friend
When all is lost so suddenly?
What then do their actions impart
When their soul rises heavenly?
Do they all get washed together
In the seas of eternity?
If a life's light never burns out
And our actions can split the seas
Then worlds can ascend to heaven
And time will keep the memories
We can truly grasp the concept
Of a life lived for Him fully
For I know we shall meet again
And shall rejoice eternally

Musings of the Northern Poet
These Stained Marks

From plants and trees
I make my pleas
In these stained marks

They stop to glance
At this small chance
Of these remarks

For if in fact
We could retract
The time we spend

Would we return
To watch it burn
Or to amend

But trees must grow
Their path is slow
An ancient sage

These eyes see through
What's left of you
Consumed by rage

We must press on
Or hope is gone
In paper stains

For words could crush
This artist's brush
'til none remains

Matthew E Nordin

To a Nettle Friend

A nettle tugged at my clothes here
He wanted me to stay I fear
For though I am writing
The crowds are inviting
To come and join in with the cheer

I tried to wrestle him away
But he is still wanting to play
And now I start to see
That I won't get him free
So on my mind he'll cling today

Warming into Renaissance

As the frosts of winter melt
The joints move where warmth is felt
Feet shift to wandering state
Hibernated bones stand straight
The fire burning in their eyes
Shrugs off the colder disguise
Now focused on something grand
Now fixed on the task at hand
His hands brace themselves to fly
Hearts leaping above the sky
He gathers his friends and grins
The renaissance now begins

What Makes a Warrior?

What makes a warrior strong?
Is it one who lives to fight
Even when the days get long
To battle 'til all is right?
Is it fear of his anger
That drives others to follow?
Is one who helps a stranger
The one who leads tomorrow?
Do the weapons make the man
Or does the man become one?
Is it marked by those who can
And makes sure justice is done?
Is it the one who can fall
And yet his love still sustains?
Warriors sacrifice all
Until only peace remains

Matthew E Nordin
Wizard of Words

Though I've debated with scholars
Held my feet with brawlers
I'm not of the cloth or the sword
I'm a wizard of words
Enchanting all who would come by
And listen for a while
My pen is not meant to offend
But to make a life smile
Words to give strength to warriors
And soften the hard heart
They can traverse every distance
With courage to impart
Reminding us of days gone by
Hoping for tomorrow
My words are meant to inspire and
Bring you out of sorrow
For though they may not be so grand
As from a wealthy man
They are here to bring you some peace
And let your heart release

Musings of the Northern Poet

Conclusion

My Mumbled Mind

I feel as if my mumbled mind
Has been engulfed in words and rhyme
No more have I the time to write
Before a new poem takes flight
Then ignoring my lovely cup
My mind drifts away to look up
I move past the day's scorching heat
For the sun exposes bare feet
Whose warmth slowly consumes our skin
And desires to make our heads spin
But clouds can cover its bright stare
They blow the breeze that doesn't care
I dare not ask where their thoughts go
For they are often high and low
Yet the sun seems to get its way
Disrupting any dreary day
Forcing the flowers to open
Their safe coverings are broken
What better way for them to live?
Showing an image to outlive
The fragile time they are given
Such is true for the forgiven
We show the mark of Creator
A Love and Beauty that's greater

Musings of the Northern Poet

Perhaps we lust for earthly things
When flesh cannot hear what soul sings
Although we were formed in the sand
The heart should not be stuck on land
It must rise up beyond the stars
Where it is pure and no sin mars
To release the hope that's repressed
And in those moments it finds rest
The softest images appear
That causes the spirit to cheer
Such dreams are sweet of love's embrace
But sweeter to wake by love's face
For in that waking moment's bliss
Dreams become real with a slight kiss
And in those moments the heart bends
To love's endless song it transcends
For what is life if lived alone
In this short time on this great stone?
Shadows do not make a good friend
They will often leave at day's end
But even dark is not just one
Others are hidden by the Sun
For in the darkness there is Light
And joyful day can break the night
When we find the Eternal Days
Then our spirits can fully praise
The love that pierces to our soul
Emptying self but making whole
Truth that shakes the highest places
And consumes our heart in graces
The touch of Divine providence
Going beyond our circumstance
Lifting us above planet's reach
Giving us new words of right speech
Until the stars stop to wonder
At the sound of mankind's thunder

Matthew E Nordin

That reflects the Creator's voice
Revealing the hope of a choice
Yet as we remain in this form
Until our bodies are all worn
We must face each day that's unknown
Knowing we will not be alone
But I fear I made my pen sore
And my muse has started to bore
Just give me a fresh cup of tea
So I can end this poetry

If you've enjoyed this book, please consider leaving a review and find Matthew's other works on Amazon:

SHADOWS OF ELEANOR

HOLLOWS OF THE NOX
A young scholar discovers a book of ancient sorcery. It challenges his understanding of magic and beacons him to embark upon a journey to find the source of its power.

AWAKENING THE STRICKEN
At the fringes of the elven kingdom, a young sorceress works on perfecting her mother's spells. Yet an evil force may be stronger than her desire to court one of the guards.

THE SALTY ELEANOR
An alchemist born to a blacksmith finds his passion in the earth's elements. Everything changes when he meets someone more enchanting than his weapons.

PASSAGE OF THE FAE
Escaping his pirate captors, a young poet travels to a place near the fae. But falling in love with one could disrupt their realms—if the worlds weren't already shattering.

THE PYCROFT UNIVERSE

THE PYCROFT PARTICLE
Doctor Patricia Pycroft is set to revolutionize the travel industry with the discovery of teleportation. When strange occurrences happen, her work and faith are questioned.

PYCROFT CONTINUUM
A collection of short stories releasing soon.

ABOUT THE AUTHOR

Matthew E. Nordin is a speculative fiction writer and a Midwestern traveler. He is secretly formulating a series of fantasy novels with a dash of science fiction tales to spice things up. His love of renaissance faires, conventions, and writing workshops have spurred his passion for setting his thoughts into print.

He met his wife while performing with the newly renamed group: Scenery Changes. Together, they specialize in improv comedy shows & acting workshops; creating artistic works & writing; living a simple life & most of all, having fun!

Join in their adventures at
www.scenerychanges.com

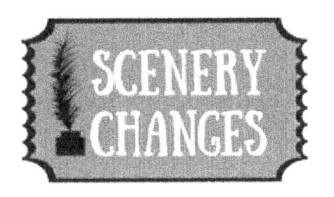

Stage & Scene & In-Between